THE
NONPROFIT
MILLIONAIRE

Doing Good Doesn't Mean Doing Bad Financially

To Greg,

Thanks for your support and leadership in my transition to the "largest Y in the world!"

Rich

G.M. "RICK" HOPKINS

Copyright © 2015 G.M. "Rick" Hopkins

First Edition

All rights reserved.

No part of this publication may be reproduced, stored in a retrieval system or transmitted in any form or by any means, electronic, mechanical, photocopying, recording, scanning or otherwise, except under the terms of the Copyright, Designs and Patents Act 1988 or under the terms of a license issued by the Copyright Licensing Agency Ltd.

ISBN: 978-0-9855552-3-8

Book Cover Design & Layout by PIXEL eMarketing INC.

Legal Disclaimer

The publisher and the author make no representations or warranties with respect to the accuracy or completeness of the contents of this work and specifically disclaim all warranties, including without limitation warranties of fitness for a particular purpose. Financial strategies in this book should be reviewed and approved by your CPA or financial advisor prior to implementation and do not guarantee specific results. No warranty maybe created or extended by sales or promotional materials. The advice and strategies contained herein may not be suitable for every situation. Furthermore the author is not responsible for your taxes and all financial scenarios presented in the book are not guarantees of income.

Neither the publisher nor the author shall be liable for damages arising here from. The fact that an organization or website is referred to in this work as a citation and/or a potential source of further information does not mean that the author or the publisher endorses the information the organization or website it may provide or recommendations it may make.

Further, readers should be aware that Internet websites listed in this work may have changed or disappeared between when this work was written and when it is read.

DEDICATIONS

Are you a *"Do-Gooder?"* If so, this book is dedicated to you.

A *do-gooder* is someone who works hard to do "good work" in the community; but is "paid badly" for his or her trouble. I am referring not only to **nonprofit professionals** here; but also, to our kindred **social sector professionals** such as teachers, first responders, social workers, nurses, lower level government employees, etc. You do what you do in order to serve and support other people... not to get rich. However, your commitment to "doing good" shouldn't automatically consign you to a lifetime of "doing bad" financially. Did you know that nonprofit and social sector professionals are among the *lowest paid*, *highest taxed*, and most *in debt* segment of our workforce? That explains a lot, doesn't it?

I hereby give you permission to be just a *little bit selfish;* and to put yourself and your family above others for a change. I empower you to live well right now; while positioning yourself to retire someday on your own terms—without having to lower your standard of living or having to work a job until the day you die. You deserve at least that.

ACKNOWLEDGMENTS

I wish to acknowledge *Mr. Ivey Stokes,* visionary founder of myEcon, Inc., for sharing with me the power of the concept of *"Personal Financial Success."* His unwavering efforts to empower others to take charge of their own personal economy, along with the guidance and support of my financial mentors, executive vice presidents, *Spencer LaCapra* and *Keith Tucker,* inspired me to take up the mantle and reclaim control of my own money.

Additionally, I want to acknowledge my lovely and talented wife, Odessa Hopkins, who inspired me to apply the concepts gleaned from my experience as an entrepreneur in a way that is relevant and applicable to the nonprofit and social sector genre. I borrowed liberally from her trademarked *"Millionaire Hustle Manifesto"* in my attempt to communicate the benefits of the "millionaire mindset," and how to use it to raise the quality of life for nonprofit and social sector professionals everywhere.

ABOUT THE AUTHOR

Rick Hopkins is a 35 year nonprofit senior executive, entrepreneur, coach, speaker, and Amazon #1 bestselling author. His first book, **"Nonprofit Doesn't Mean No Profit,"** explored the subject of *fiscal sustainability* within nonprofit organizations from an *entrepreneurial perspective*. A long time ago, someone started a nasty rumor that nonprofit organizations were not supposed to make a profit; that somehow losing money was an expectation of nonprofit status. Hopkins points out that, to his way of thinking, *no profit* eventually means *out of business*… even for nonprofit organizations.

In this sequel, **"The Nonprofit Millionaire,"** Hopkins challenges yet another nasty rumor; this time, about nonprofit professionals and their personal finances. He debunks the myth that because you work for a nonprofit organization, *you are predestined to struggle financially in your personal life.* Hopkins does not believe the term "nonprofit millionaire" to be an oxymoron. He contends that living comfortably, even for those with moderate incomes, is imminently achievable.

CONTENTS

PREFACE: The Millionaire Myth 1

INTRODUCTION: Take Home What You Make Home 7
   Things That Make You Go… Hmmm 12

CHAPTER 1: Break The Cycle Of Pain 15
   Cycle of Pain – Stage One................. 18
   Cycle of Pain – Stage Two 20
   "I Will Gladly Pay You Tuesday For A Hamburger Today" 22
   Cycle of Pain – Stage Three 23

CHAPTER 2: Three Steps To Financial Success .27
   Step One: Take Home What You Make Home 31
   Step Two: Shield Your Job Income 34
   Step Three: No More Sucker's Bets 36

CHAPTER 3: **The Power Of Income Shifting.... 39**
The First Income Shift................. 44
The Second Income Shift 46
The Third Income Shift................ 47
The Final Income Shift 49

CHAPTER 4: **Strategic Business Venture 53**

CHAPTER 5: **The Magic Of The W-4............61**
Take Back Your Tax 64
The Next Level....................... 67
She Looks Like A Million Dollars.......... 71

CHAPTER 6: **How Tax Deductions Really work . 75**
Driving Miss Daisy To The Bank 78
There Is No Place Like Home............. 81
If Ya Gotta Go, Ya Gotta Go! 82
Another Day, Another Quarter............ 84
Stick Out Your Tongue And Say…Ahhhhh .. 86

CHAPTER 7: **The Job Isn't Over Until The Paperwork Is Done...................... 89**
The Form 1040 Schedule A............... 92
The Form 1040 Schedule C............... 93

CHAPTER 8: Choosing Your SBV 95
Firing Your Boss 101

CHAPTER 9: The SBV Academy Online 105
Level One Coaching 109
Level Two Coaching 110
Level Three Coaching 111
Video Coaching Program 112

CONCLUSION: Sword & Shield Mindset 117

REFERENCES 123

PREFACE

THE MILLIONAIRE MYTH

"I don't know much about being a millionaire; but I'll bet I'd be darling at it."
DOROTHY PARKER

I will bet you never thought you would hear the words *"nonprofit"* and *"millionaire"* in the same sentence, did you?

When you think millionaire, you probably envision someone like the person pictured above. *Seldom, if ever, does the image of a nonprofit or social sector professional come to mind*; yet, in reality, they exist all around us. They fly unnoticed under the radar because they aren't compelled to wear the latest fashions, drink fine wines or drive expensive luxury automobiles. Instead, they put their money to work securing their future; not posturing to impress you. I know quite a few of these *undercover millionaires* myself; and whether you realize it or not—so do you!

It's perfectly understandable why the image of a nonprofit millionaire is not top of mind for most of us. After all, approximately half of America's millionaires got there as a result of businesses they own, not by working a job. Another third made it through inheritance and investments, and some from good old fashioned hard work. Somewhere within the remaining 10% to 12% resides the unpretentious subculture of undercover millionaires. This small, elite group of hard-working wage-earning employees got there primarily through the use of *proven financial strategies* readily available to everyone—the kind you will learn from this book.

Over time, we have romanticized and grossly exaggerated what it means to be a millionaire; so, first, let's define what a millionaire is.

> *Technically, a "millionaire" is someone who owns an asset or assets that generate around $8,500 a month (the amount of interest paid on a million dollars); or who possesses some tangible object or entity valued at $1,000,000 or more.*

Here's the good news... earning a million dollars is really not all that difficult. *Did you know that if you make just $10 an hour over the course of your working life, you will easily earn over a million dollars?* The bad news is that, for reasons we will discuss in detail soon, you lose a third of that million dollars right off the top; and another third attempting to compensate financially for your initial loss.

Do the math—this means that *you have been trying in vain to live on only one third of your lifetime earnings*. No wonder you're broke all the time! The underlying problem here is that most of us simply don't understand *how money really works*. It's not your fault, though. In school, they go to great lengths to teach you about numbers; conversely, they expend very little effort to educate you on the intricacies of making money. Algebra and trigonometry are great in and of themselves; but you can't spend them.

The truth is, if you make $50,000 a year, you can't afford NOT to be a nonprofit millionaire! If you had to retire today; you would need a 401-K, IRA or some other income generating asset worth about $500,000 to pay a monthly income equal to your current salary. If you plan to retire in twenty years or so, given the anticipated rate of inflation and escalating cost of living, you would need to own an asset worth around $1,000,000 just to maintain your current standard of living. Otherwise, you would probably have to continue working during your "golden years."

Your money works hard out there twenty four hours a day, three hundred sixty five days a year, making someone rich—unfortunately, *that someone is probably not you*. But it doesn't have to be that way. Implementation of the proven financial strategies in this book will give you back control of your own money; as well as the personal and financial freedom to live life on your terms.

G.M. "Rick" Hopkins

INTRODUCTION

TAKE HOME WHAT YOU MAKE HOME

"You must pay taxes, but there's no law that says that you have to leave a tip."
UNKNOWN

Allow me to begin with a true story as told to me by a first-responder friend of mine from Washington, DC:

> Upon arriving at the scene of a terrible automobile accident, he found a teenage girl in the wreckage of her car patiently waiting for help to arrive. Given the circumstances, she seemed quite calm and in good spirits. *He immediately noticed that her left arm had been completely severed during the crash*—yet she seemed oblivious to the fact. When I asked how this could be, he explained that the human brain has self-defense mechanisms in place to keeping us from going into shock and, perhaps, dying as a result.
>
> Surprisingly, the young lady was not upset about her arm because she was completely unaware it was missing. Her brain had instinctively shut down the pain centers in her shoulder, and would not allow her to even look in the general direction of her grave injury. This was fortunate for her because had she looked, she surely would have panicked, gone into a state of shock and died!

So what's all that got to do with becoming a *nonprofit millionaire*? Stay with me here. I promise you, I do have a point.

When is the last time you looked at your paycheck; I mean *really* looked at it in detail? Of course, you look at the *net pay* section because you know that's what you will actually take home. Seldom do you bother to look at the *gross pay* amount, the fixed expenses or the taxes taken out. What's the point anyway, right? *It is what it is.* Similar to what occurred with the young lady in the car accident; this is an example of your brain protecting you from having to deal with a reality for which you are simply unprepared or unwilling to face.

If you really thought about how much of your hard earned money is taken from your paycheck each month, you probably would experience at least one of three probable reactions: anger, frustration or perhaps shock. Now step back and ask yourself, *"What if you had full access to your entire paycheck?"* That's *not* a rhetorical question, by the way. Imagine for a moment how your life would change if you could take home your *gross pay* instead of just your *net pay*. All of a sudden, winning the lottery is not your only option to drastically improve your financial situation.

If you could just *"Take Home What You Make Home,"* it would change your life; and the way you think about money forever. This concept is the first step of what I call my **Three Steps to Financial Success** process, the underlying framework for most of the instructional content of this book. The concept itself is quite simple:

> "If you <u>make</u> $50,000 a year then you should <u>take home</u> $50,000… not $35,000 after Uncle Sam takes his cut."

Interesting concept, wouldn't you agree? Fortunately, it <u>can</u> be done. However, a *paradigm shift* of this magnitude requires your willingness to look at things much differently. As a result of seeing things differently, you should be empowered to act differently. *Trying to change is not enough.* As Master Yoda from the Star Wars movies said: "Try not. Do or do not—there is no try."

Unlike the organizations we work for that get lots of financial support from the government, business community, foundations and private individuals in the form of tax exemptions, grants, and tax deductible donations; *we, as wage earning employees, get no such consideration.* While we certainly don't begrudge our employers this support; it hardly seems fair that we, the ones in the trenches actually doing the great work that justifies it, are overlooked.

That being said, I have never been one to play the *"Ain't It Awful?"* game. Instead, I prefer to focus on solving the problem. To get to the right solution, you must first learn to ask the right questions. Instead of asking "Why do I have no money?" ask yourself "Why is my money making *other people* rich and not me?" Another key question to ask yourself is "What is my largest recurring monthly expense?" Like most people, you probably assume the answer to be your *home* or *automobile*. Well, the good news is that you asked yourself the right question this time—the bad news is that you got the *wrong answer*! The correct answer is *taxes*. For most Americans, income taxes are far and away their largest expense.

Think about it. *You lose a third of your income to taxes*; if you include sales taxes, property taxes and other specialty taxes, it's probably closer to 50%! My father used to tell me that *if I ever lost money, the best place to find it is the same place I lost it*—for most people, that place is taxes. So let's start there!

Things That Make You Go... Hmmm

Why does Uncle Sam tax 100% of your paycheck right off the top, while a business owner is only taxed on money left over after he pays all his expenses—up to and including paying himself?

Doesn't seem fair, does it? Did you know:

- If a nonprofit or social sector professional makes $50,000 a year, he or she is immediately taxed on all $50,000.
- If a traditional business owner also makes $50,000, the rules are quite different. For example, if he or she spends $40,000 on business expenses including paying his or her own salary—only the remaining $10,000 would be taxed!
- Both individuals made the same amount of money and are taxed at the same rate; however, the wage earner pays significantly more tax than the business owner.

Does this mean that everyone with a job should abruptly quit tomorrow and start a business? Of course not! Should you rise up against the IRS? That would be unwise. I propose that you not *rail against the system*, but work within it to achieve your fiscal objectives. Your overarching goal is to make Uncle Sam your *financial partner*, not your adversary. In order to do that, you must first position yourself to be seen by him as just that.

This is what traditional millionaires do. Prospective *nonprofit millionaires* would do well to emulate them. The rewards of this strategy are well worth the effort. In return, Uncle Sam will grant you "cash in your pocket" in the form of *tax exemptions*, *tax deductions* and *tax credits* with which to protect your job income.

CHAPTER 1

BREAK THE CYCLE OF PAIN

"Once you have eliminated the impossible, whatever remains, however improbable, must be the truth."
SIR ARTHUR CONAN DOYLE

I truly believe that God has a special place in Heaven for *nonprofit and social sector professionals*. No one works longer or harder than we do; or more often puts the needs of others ahead of our own. How much is a teacher worth who inspires and educates young minds; or a first responder who puts life and limb on the line every day? What about the social worker who works with the homeless; or the YMCA director who cares for your kids after school and during the summer while you have to work? What is their monetary value? Not that much, apparently—according to our paychecks, anyway.

People who do what we do will probably never be rich; but why must we struggle so hard financially just to provide the basic necessities for ourselves and our families? *We mistakenly believe our problem is that we don't make enough money*; but that's not it. The money we earn manages quite well to make plenty of *other people* rich. We can either go on making Uncle Sam, the banks and the insurance companies rich; or we can decide to learn how to put our own money to work for us.

Our financial issues are derived less from how much money we earn, or *do not* earn; and more from how much of it we actually get to take home. Of course, what we do with it is important as well. As a group, nonprofit and social sector professionals are nothing if not resourceful; we simply find a way to "make it work." That's just who we are. As a result, many of us suffer from an all too common financial phenomenon known as the "**Cycle of Pain**."

The symptoms are easily identified:

1. You have no money.
2. You are in debt.
3. You have no savings or investments.

If the organization that employs you operated like this, it would soon be out of business. If you performed on your job this way, you would soon be out of a job. So what makes you think you can operate this way at home and still be able to survive financially and provide for your family?

Cycle of Pain - Stage One

So, why do you have no money? It certainly isn't because you live an extravagant lifestyle. You don't own a mansion on a hill, drive expensive luxury automobiles or have a gambling addiction. So why are you having so much trouble making ends meet?

Once you have eliminated all the *usual excuses* for why you are broke all the time, you will discover that the answer was right there in front of you, hiding in plain sight. After you stop eating out quite so often, and switch to buying your groceries wholesale and cooking at home; after you realize that you don't actually need 275 cable TV channels to be happy; after you turn down your thermostats and restrict your movie going to matinees only… don't be surprised to find yourself still in the same situation. Why? Silly rabbit—it is because *you can't cure a disease by treating only the symptoms.*

It is no different than what frequently occurs in the workplace. When you experience significant shortfalls in the company budget, *you can't solve the problem by simply cutting back on paper clips or removing the coffee pot from the employee lounge.* Ultimately, you may have to lay off staff. It sucks, I know; but the truth is that *people costs* are an organization's largest expense—usually around 60% to 65% of the total operation. Therefore, any major bottom line adjustments would have to involve your largest expense to some extent.

Similarly, in your personal life, your largest expenses are *taxes* and *debt.* The truth is *you don't have any money because you are overpaying your taxes.* Over time, however, you just became numb, accepted it all and stopped asking yourself *"Who is this F.I.C.A. guy and his pals—and why are they allowed to take so much of my paycheck?"* Eventually, you did what all humans tend to do in tough situations... you simply adapted and moved on. That was the <u>wrong question</u>, anyway! A better question is: *"Why am I paying so much more tax than other people who make much more money that I do?"*

Cycle of Pain – Stage Two

The other primary reason you have no money is because you are in debt up to your eyeballs. What's worse is that you're probably not quite sure how you got there. Suddenly, you find that you can no longer pay off your credit card balances in full each month; opting increasingly for making just the minimum monthly payment. No big deal, right? In addition to that, you also find yourself paying late fees on most of your monthly bills. So what? It's just a few extra bucks here and there, right? That's what you tell yourself, anyway. When this begins to happen more and more often—you have officially arrived at Stage Two!

There is another reason why you are in debt. *You are probably in debt because of trying unsuccessfully to compensate for the money you lost to taxes!* In reality, you are still spending $50,000, even though you actually take home only around $35,000. You don't believe me? Look closely at your interest debt statements: your credit cards, mortgage, car loan, student loan, etc. *Don't be surprised if you find their total is roughly equal to the amount of your tax loss!* That's right, not only are you losing a third of your income to taxes; you are also losing another third to interest debt! No wonder you can't seem to get ahead—you are trying to live on only a third of your income. Yes, I am going to keep repeating this until it sinks in.

If there is a silver lining in this dark cloud, it's that debt is 100% under your control. However, managing your debt does require you to make some tough choices; and not always a choice between good and bad, as illustrated by the following:

> *A hit man took his victim to the edge of a cliff, put a gun to his head and told him "jump or I will blow your head off." The victim sighed and said, "I guess I don't have a choice." The hit man snickered and said, "of course you have a choice… just not a very good one!"*

You can <u>choose</u> not to swipe that credit card because you know full well that you don't have enough money in your checking account. You can *choose* to redirect money you now spend on *liabilities* and apply it to acquiring *assets*. But the most impactful choice you can make is to *choose* to *educate yourself financially*, regarding how to pay less in taxes, get out of debt and free up money to invest. Then, be sure to pass this invaluable knowledge on to your children. Paying it forward in this manner is the foundation of how the wealthy build *generational wealth*.

"I Will Gladly Pay You Tuesday For A Hamburger Today"

For those of you who do not remember; or perhaps who may not have been born yet, that famous quote is by a character named *Wimpy* from the old *Popeye the Sailor* cartoons of my youth. Wimpy loved hamburgers, but he was always broke. Because he had no money, Wimpy would constantly try to borrow money from his friends to buy a hamburger with the promise that he would pay them back next Tuesday.

I assume that Wimpy must have had a job, although it was never mentioned; and that Tuesday was his payday. In retrospect, it was a moot point as no one ever lent him any money anyway. But what if credit cards had been around back then? If so, how much debt do you suppose Wimpy would have found himself in due to his lack of financial discipline? Wimpy would be right at home today because we have become a society that would gladly pay you next Tuesday for pretty much anything if they can have what they want today.

Are you like Wimpy? Credit is NOT your friend… always remember that!

Cycle of Pain – Stage Three

Unfortunately, the Cycle of Pain has not yet run its course. In the third and final stage, beware of what I call the "Sucker's Bet." *A sucker's bet is when you are led to believe that something is in your best interest when it isn't.* You have no savings or investments because just when you start to get a little bit ahead, along comes a sucker's bet disguised as something good and puts you back to square one.

A perfect example is a *bank savings account* that pays you interest on your money at a lower rate than the rate of inflation; thereby guaranteeing that *your money will be worth less when you take it out than when you put it in.* We are taught early on that saving money in a bank is a good thing. In reality, with bank savings, you are not much better off than if you had stuffed your cash in a mattress or buried it in the back yard. At least, if you had done so, *nobody else* would have been getting rich off your money instead of you.

Think for a moment how a bank makes its money. It takes your cash in exchange for a promise to keep it safe and guarantees to compensate you at a ridiculously low rate of interest for your trouble. What happens next? Does your money just sit there in the bank waiting for you to come back for it? Of course not! That money is out the door nearly as quickly as you are. The bank uses your money to pay its *own* bills, to lower its *own* debt, to invest in its *own* future; additionally it loans your money out at incredibly high interest rates… all while paying you a ridiculously low interest rate.

Banks and other "reputable" financial institutions invest your money with top money management companies like Fidelity, Vanguard and T. Rowe Price earning 8% to 12% on average. Additionally, they lend your money out at even higher interest rates, often upwards of 22%. Then they turn around and pay you 1% to 2% interest on your money. You fall victim to sucker's bets because you fail to recognize them for what they really are… this is what *makes* them sucker's bets in the first place.

I wish bank savings was the only sucker's bet you had to look out for. There are many others, and we will address some of the most dangerous ones throughout the book. Don't set up camp permanently within the economic "**Cycle of Pain**." If so, you will continue to have *no money*, the credit trap will keep you *in debt* and you still have *no savings or investments* to fund your retirement.

NOTES

CHAPTER 2

THREE STEPS TO FINANCIAL SUCCESS

"Know the enemy and know yourself,
and in a hundred battles you will
be victorious."
SUN TZU, THE ART OF WAR

In Eastern philosophy, you have the *yin* and the *yang*; which represent the two complimentary forces that make up all aspects and phenomena of life. Examples are all around us: good and evil, black and white, male and female, rich and poor, young and old, wet and dry, heaven and hell—the list is endless. If the **Cycle of Pain** is the *yin*—then my **Three Steps to Financial Success** is the *yang*. As you might suspect, it's no coincidence that the *three financial strategies* of the latter match up quite nicely with the *three stages* of the former.

First, let's recap the "Three Steps" collectively before exploring the finer details of each individually:

1. Take Home What You Make Home
2. Shield Your Job Income
3. No More Sucker's Bets

Right now your money busy is making *somebody* rich; unfortunately, that somebody probably is not you. Given this, your first objective should be to *take back control of your own money*. There are lots of obstacles preventing you from doing this. Your two most formidable adversaries are *high taxes* and *interest debt*; this is why we have to deal with them on the front end. Doing so gives you the initiative and puts you in control of your *current state*, allowing you to live your desired lifestyle now while you are still working.

Someday, however, you will want to be able to stop working, without having to lower your standard of living. This represents controlling your *future state*. Inflation and less than ideal cashflow management are your key obstacles here, making you extremely vulnerable to what I call "sucker's bets;" sometimes known as the "old okey-doke." Failure to control your future state will result in you possibly never being able to retire; or perhaps having to work a job until the day you die.

Step One: Take Home What You Make Home

If you make $50,000 a year, you should take home $50,000—not $35,000 after Uncle Sam takes his cut. The problem starts with the W-4 Tax Withholding Form. You are already familiar with this form; or, at least, you should be. You filled one out for every job you have ever had. The W-4 is where you claim your *allowances* for the year. Therein, as they say, lies the rub. Most people get it wrong because they have no idea what an allowance is.

An allowance is simply a mathematical calculation that determines how much tax your employer withholds from your paycheck.

The IRS' own website points out that 80% of Americans overpay our taxes, simply because we fill out their *W-4* incorrectly. This is the slush fund from which Uncle Sam pays out tax refunds. We will talk more about them in a later chapter when we discuss "sucker's bets" in detail.

The next useful tool to help you *take home what you make home* is the tax deduction. Unfortunately, as a wage earning employee, you qualify for very few of them. This includes 90% of the American workforce. Later you will learn how to access literally hundreds of lucrative tax deductions currently not available to you. The best part is that it is all legal, moral, ethical; and more importantly, according to IRS guidelines. By correcting your W-4 Tax Withholding Form and skillfully utilizing loopholes and tax deductions, you will be able to reclaim most, if not all, of your income lost to taxes.

Now let me be perfectly clear… *I don't advocate avoiding paying your taxes!* I believe in paying every penny you owe in taxes… but not a penny more. You have more control over how much tax you actually owe than you probably realize. The problem is that *Uncle Sam always takes more than he entitled to up front; and then just sits back and waits for you to come back for it.* He knows that most people won't bother to do it because they either don't know how, or are too intimidated by the IRS to do so. Don't be like most people. Learn the financial rules of engagement and take back what's yours.

Did you know that income tax was never supposed to be permanent? It was invoked in 1862, and was intended to be a *temporary measure* to help support the Civil War effort—and it just never went away! Actually, that's not true; it did go away for a couple of years. In 1895 the US Supreme Court ruled income tax to be unconstitutional; but it didn't take long for Uncle Sam to overturn that ruling and get his sticky fingers back in our wallets.

If you are looking for *fairness*, the tax codes are not the place to find it. *It's a fact that even though the wealthy make more money, they pay proportionately less in taxes.* This doesn't happen by accident; the wealthy are purposeful in their efforts to minimize their taxable income. You should do the same.

Step Two: Shield Your Job Income

Job income is one of our government's largest sources of tax revenue, even though wage earners don't even come close to representing the largest portion of this country's wealth. This is the veiled reason why we hear so much from politicians about the importance of *job creation* and putting Americans back to work. In reality, it isn't necessarily because more jobs is good for the people; but more so because it is good for tax revenues.

In the final analysis, there are primarily three ways that money is earned in America, and each is taxed differently:

1. W-2 or Job Income
2. 1099 or Business Income
3. Investment Income (i.e. interest, dividends, capital gains)

Of course, each has its own distinct advantages and disadvantages. While W-2 and 1099 income both *appear* to be taxed at the same rate; in reality, nothing could be further from the truth. 100% of W-2 income is taxed up front; while 1099 income is not taxed until after all relevant expenses are deducted, up to and including paying yourself.

One way to look at it is that with W-2 income you *spend what is left over after taxes*. With 1099 income, you are *taxed on what is left over after spending*. With 1099 income, under the right circumstances, it is possible to owe no tax at all. What a deal! Investment income, by contrast, benefits from the lowest tax rates of all… usually in the single digits. I am reminded of something my mentor once told me: *"Money is always taxed less than labor."*

The key to *shielding your job income* lies in being able to access the tax advantages of business income and to apply them in such a way as to offset the extreme *tax disadvantages* of W-2 job income. I coach my clients on a financial strategy called "Income Shifting," which guides them through the transition from W-2 income to 1099 income to investment income… while minimizing the downsides and maximizing the upsides of each. Fortunately, Congress has enacted tax legislation that, under certain conditions, allows you to do just that. The rules, however, are quite specific, and require you to keep good tax records; but this is a small price to pay for the financial benefit afforded you.

Step Three: No More Sucker's Bets

We previously defined a "sucker's bet" as *something that appears to be in your best interest but isn't*. That's what makes them so dangerous… you don't see them coming. I have already mentioned a few of my "favorites," such as the bank savings account, the income tax refund, predatory mortgages and taking on a second job. Some are more obvious; like getting a "free trial" of some product or service, but only after giving them your credit card information that will be charged later if you forget to cancel. How about buying a new car with a high interest long term auto loan, and having it depreciate 20% to 30% as soon as you drive it off the lot?

Financial education is the key to not falling prey to wasting money on any number of sucker's bets. How we *spend* our money is just as important as how we *save* and *invest* it. Most people buy luxuries with their salaries; or even worse, *on credit*… a major reason why they are in debt in the first place. Of course, the wealthy buy luxuries too, lots of them; but they tend to buy them with *profits* from their businesses, investments and revenue producing assets. That new Jaguar that Skipper or Buffy is driving was probably paid for with the profits from some real estate deal, or the sale of a business; certainly not with a high interest auto loan.

If something that *appears* to make you more money, but at the same time *increases your tax liability*; or if something causes you to exceed your available financial resources resulting in additional interest charges or late payment fees, it is probably a sucker's bet. Something that reduces your ability to accumulate assets that will help support you financially later on certainly qualifies as well. *Anything that diminishes your present or future fiscal sustainability through deceit or misrepresentation is definitely a sucker's bet.*

NOTES

CHAPTER 3

THE POWER OF INCOME SHIFTING

"The only difference between death and taxes is that death doesn't get worse every time Congress meets."
WILL ROGERS

Income Shifting refers to the act of strategically moving money from one income stream to another, simultaneously creating new and expanding existing cashflow channels along the way.

Mastering the concept of income shifting is one way wealthy people became wealthy in the first place—and how they will continue to be so for generations to come. This strategy should be part of every prospective nonprofit millionaire's financial toolbox. The concept is not rocket science; neither is it top secret or classified information reserved for the chosen few. It might seem that way, but only because *so few* have chosen to avail themselves of this knowledge.

Income shifting is based on the premise that there are basically three ways that income is earned in this country:

1. **W-2 Income** ~ salaries and wages from a job
2. **1099 Income** ~ business and contractor income
3. **Investment Income** ~ dividends, interest earnings, appreciation, capital gains, etc.

There are, of course, advantages and disadvantages to each. Subsequently, *most people tend to focus, almost exclusively, on salary as their primary source of income.* Why? It's probably because we simply were not taught any other way; I know I wasn't. Don't blame your parents, though. *While we cannot be held responsible for what we have been taught; we are absolutely accountable for what we choose now to learn.* If I had known about money in my early thirties what I know now; I would be comfortably retired with a lot more cash in my pocket!

W-2 income is, basically, the money you earn on your job. It is the highest taxed of the three revenue sources at 28% to 33%. You often hear me refer to losing a third of our income to taxes; this is where that particular statistic comes from. While this high tax rate is certainly not ideal, what's even worse is <u>when</u> the tax is actually applied. For W-2s, tax is deducted from your salary right off the top. You never see it, so you never miss it—that's the theory anyway—I, for one, certainly missed mine.

This is not to imply that W-2 income is bad—on the contrary. There is much to be said for a steady paycheck. I have awakened may a Friday morning with a smile on my face because it was payday. *As a wage earning employee, you must realize and accept that you will never be paid what you are worth—you will only be paid what the job is worth.* Your value is determined by someone else, your ability to earn more is limited, and your tax burden will be excessive. In order to significantly increase your job income—you will probably have to get a better job.

1099 income is money you earn as a business owner or independent contractor. *This type of income has clear advantages over its W-2 counterpart.* While it is, technically, taxed at the same rate as W-2 income—28% to 33%—special circumstances apply that reduce the net effect of considerably. This anomaly occurs because *1099 income is not taxed until the end of the year—after all applicable business expenses have been paid, up to and including paying your own salary!* By lowering your taxable income in this way, you invariably end up paying *much less* in taxes.

Soon you will be introduced to a unique financial vehicle, designed specifically for nonprofit and social sector professionals, which will allow you to write off everyday expenses—that you were going to spend money on anyway—against your W-2 income. Additionally, this vehicle can also generate significant amounts of 1099 income as well. It will change your life.

Investment income is cashflow generated from dividends, stocks and bonds, real estate, interest earnings, capital gains, and other "passive" types of income. This type of income is taxed at less than 10%. Once again, I am reminded that *"money will always be taxed less than labor."* Think for a moment about the representatives we send to Washington DC to supposedly represent our interests. Do they come from _labor_, or do they come from _money_? Now look at our tax laws. Do they favor labor, or do they favor money? Enough said.

The First Income Shift

The first income shift begins with understanding and correcting your W-4 Tax Withholding form. If you are like most people, no one ever sat down with you and explained how to fill it out correctly. As a result, 80% of Americans over pay their taxes every year. Why didn't HR explain to you how to correctly fill out your W-4 form? Believe it or not, it is actually *against the law* for them to advise you on your personal taxes. The issue stems from liability issues resulting from employees playing *fast and loose* with adjusting their allowances up and down with fraudulent intent.

The key words here are "fraudulent intent." When challenged by the IRS, employees often claimed that they acted on the advice of the HR department. As usual, rather than opt for improved communication and training on the subject, most companies simply refuse to give employees any advice whatsoever. After all, companies have nothing to lose when their employees over pay their taxes. *If you overpay your taxes, the worst that can happen is that you get a tax refund, right?* Wrong again.

A tax refund means that, like it or not, you are now in the *banking business*—the business of giving Uncle Sam an interest-free loan with your hard-earned tax money. If you really were in the banking business; to be blunt, you would suck at it! Think about it. *Would any self-respecting bank loan you money and let you pay it back a year later without paying any interest on it?* I don't think so! But that is, literally, what you are doing when you get your tax refund every year. Imagine what you could have done with your money if you had access to it all year instead of Uncle Sam. You could have done the same things Uncle Sam did with your money: pay bills, lower debt and invest.

Correcting your W-4 Tax Withholding Form is not difficult. All you have to do is *read the instructions* and *answer the questions*. The problem is that the questions were written by lawyers—enough said. You have to break them down, similar to how you learned to deconstruct a compound sentence in grade school. *Only focus on the part that actually applies to you and your particular situation.* Be sure to take all the allowances you have coming to you. Remember, if you are getting $2,000 to $4,000 a year in back tax refunds; you are simply not claiming enough allowances. If you end up owing at the end of the year, then you took *too many* allowances.

The Second Income Shift

The next income shift occurs when you decide to leave the *banking business* and enter the *cashflow management business*. This time, you are in the business of creating new cashflow. Not a problem—you actually created your first new cashflow stream when you corrected your W-4 Tax Withholding Form. Have you ever heard of the "four point play" in basketball?

> The *four point play* occurs when your opponent misses an easy layup, a sure two points; and your team gets the rebound and immediately scores an easy two-pointer at the opposite end of the court. The two points your opponent *didn't* score combines with the two points your team *did* score resulting in a positive four point swing in your team's favor.
>
> When you correct your W-4, you essentially

take away your *interest free loan* to Uncle Sam, and can repurpose it into a new stream of cashflow for yourself. Now what should you do with this newfound windfall? Go shopping, perhaps? If so, you haven't heard a word I have said. Instead of *impulse spending*, perhaps you should focus on putting that money to work for you. Why not shift the newfound cashflow from your W-4 tax savings toward quickly paying down and eliminating your credit cards, short-term loans, and other high-interest debts.

By combining the money you were previously spending on debt service with your tax savings, you have, in reality, created *yet another* new cashflow stream that can be used to start a modest investment program. Now you can begin to experience the wonder that is *compound interest*. I promise, it will set you free!

The Third Income Shift

Perhaps the most exciting income shift occurs next when the full potential of your *Strategic Business Venture* is realized. You will learn all about the *SBV* in the next chapter. Up to this point you have been playing *strictly defense*. Let's not kid ourselves, *the IRS is going to get theirs*—they just don't have to get it all from you! Even Muhammad Ali in his prime could only lay back on the ropes and cover up for so long. At some point he had to come off the ropes swinging. Now it is time for you to mount your own financial *counter attack*.

Under certain circumstances, business tax deductions can be written off against your job income; *shielding it from excessive taxation* while simultaneously creating yet another significant new stream of cashflow from the *tax savings*. Congress has enacted several laws that make this possible; but it is up to you to take advantage of them. Now you can write off *appropriate percentages* of big-ticket expense items such as your *home, automobile, food, clothing, electronics, furniture, equipment*, and more… to the extent that they apply to the strategies I will teach you. Is this a loophole? Of course it is. But if it is legal, moral, ethical; and, more importantly, is in accordance with IRS guidelines and puts money back in your pocket… I say go for it!

Why not claim legitimate tax deductions for expenses you would incur *anyway*, such as an *office in the home, auto mileage, eating out, travel, internet, cell phones*, and *computers*? Do you pay your six-to-eighteen-year-old a weekly or monthly allowance? If so, why not hire them to work for you and pay them a salary up to $6,200 a year per child? Surely, they can handle routine tasks like checking your email, downloading info from the internet, cleaning your office or performing minor clerical duties for you. If you have more than one child, you can claim $6,200 per child—tax free!

This is just the tip of the tax deduction iceberg.

The Final Income Shift

The final income shift is actually more reminiscent of a rite of passage than anything else. At this point, *you are no longer working for your money—your money is now working for you.* You have successfully shifted your income from exclusively W-2—the highest tax rate with the fewest deductions—to a combination of all three primary income types. The specific revenue mix in question would, of course, vary per individual.

Congratulations! You have now been formally introduced to the overarching principles of **Smart Cashflow Management:**

- Minimizing Taxes
- Reducing Expenses
- Eliminating Debt
- Claiming Business Deductions
- Generating Business Income
- Creating Income Producing Assets

You now have the means to create six new cashflow streams from your own money. Once created, combined, and integrated into your ongoing financial strategies, this money will lay the foundation for not only building current personal wealth; but for building long term generational wealth as well. Learn these lessons well. Teach them to those you love. Let your family inherit more from you than sentimental trinkets and unpaid bills.

NOTES

CHAPTER 4
STRATEGIC BUSINESS VENTURE

"A penny saved is a penny earned."
BENJAMIN FRANKLIN

You will need a sound *financial vehicle* to drive the strategies you will learn from this book. Fortunately, I have developed such a vehicle for you, designed specifically with nonprofit and social sector professionals in mind. It is called the **Strategic Business Venture**; and I promise, it will change your life, and the way you think about money forever.

The **SBV** is aptly named because it exists only to execute specific financial strategies. It allows you to access lucrative tax advantages, previously unavailable to W-2 employees, because it meets IRS qualifications for a home based business. *The SBV is unique because, unlike a traditional business model, it is not all about earning <u>more</u> income—it is more about making <u>less</u> of your job income taxable.* Paying less in taxes frees up new cashflow with which to pay bills, get yourself out of debt and invest in your future. It is primarily for this purpose that I created the SBV.

Keep in mind that the only difference between *ordinary* and *extraordinary* is just a little *"extra."* The SBV is for those who want a little extra in their personal finances. As long as you are willing to work at it just three to four hours a week with *intent to make a profit*, you are good to go with the IRS. I don't know about you, but if I am going to do something, I *intend* to be profitable at it.

Though primarily focused on cashflow creation from tax savings and debt reduction, an SBV is quite capable of generating significant 1099 income as well. No income taxes are taken out until you file your return at year end. *You have full use of 100% of your money and only have to pay taxes after you apply all allowable business expenses—up to and including paying yourself.* What a deal! Even if you lose money, you can write it off against your W-2 income. There is no downside here.

Someday, when I am finally called to leave this Earth, I want my tombstone to read the following:

"Here lies Rick Hopkins, creator of the *Strategic Business Venture*, the financial vehicle that allowed millions of ordinary people to live comfortably during their working years; and then retire on their own terms without having to lower their standard of living."

Yeah, I know it would take a massive tombstone to hold all of that… but you get the point!

The beauty of the SBV is that you can access the tax advantages normally associated with being in business, without the hassle of actually having to run one. You are not required to sell lotions, potions, powders and pills in order to qualify with Uncle Sam as a legitimate business entity. There's no need to lease office space, hire employees, manage IT systems or devote lots of hours to it. *An SBV can be something that is fun for you, like a hobby.* In fact many hobbies work quite well as SBVs. I believe that "If it isn't your *passion*, don't make it your *profession*."

I have clients who work full time traditional jobs, but also operate SBVs based on their income producing hobbies in their free time. For example, a good friend of mine is a power company manager by day; and is also a talented artist in his own right. He sells his paintings out of his home and online. However, the money he makes selling his art pales in comparison to the tax savings he gets by using his SBV to shield his considerable job income from excessive taxation.

As a senior executive with the country's largest nonprofit organization, I earn a pretty good salary. However, *it is all W-2 income*, so Uncle Sam takes a huge chunk of it—at least he used to before I got my act together. Between New York State, New York

City and federal income tax, I could potentially lose as much as 46% of my income to taxes. By setting up an SBV and making Uncle Sam my financial partner instead of my adversary, I can now reclaim most of it *legally*, *morally* and *ethically*; but most importantly, in accordance with IRS guidelines.

You might be thinking, "Why not just take on a second job to earn extra income instead?" After all, that's what your parents did, right? And it seemed to work for them. Did it really? Maybe it seemed that way to you, but I'll bet your parents wished there had been a better way. In fact, *earning more W-2 income will not solve your financial problems…it will probably make them worse.* Ironically, the more W-2 income you make, the more tax you pay and the less you take home. This is a real world example of the *Law of Diminishing Returns* in action.

Without proper context, the *Strategic Business Venture* can be difficult to conceptualize; but as part of an overarching *smart cashflow management strategy*, it makes perfect sense. Properly utilized, it can help create new streams of cashflow from tax savings, debt elimination, and investments. *It can also convert everyday lifestyle expenses, money you were going to spend anyway, into lucrative tax deductions.* An SBV can even generate its own 1099 income if you choose to pursue this option.

In the following chapters, you will see how the SBV integrates seamlessly with the three pillars of wealth building and financial success: 1) *Minimizing Taxes*, 2) *Eliminating Debt*, and 3) *Savings & Investment*.

NOTES

CHAPTER 5

THE MAGIC OF THE W-4

"Strategy without tactics is the slowest route to victory. Tactics without strategy is the noise before defeat.
SUN TZU, THE ART OF WAR

You're probably thinking, "Here we go again with that doggone W-4 stuff—what makes it so important that you devote a whole chapter to it?" *It's important because you probably won't get this information anywhere else.* Not much is written about the W-4, and that's a shame. The IRS' own website points out that 80% of Americans overpay our taxes, simply because we fill out their *W-4 Tax Withholding Form* incorrectly. The W-4 is where you claim your *allowances* for the year. And therein, as they say, lies the rub—most people get it wrong because they have no idea of what an allowance is.

The correct number of allowances one should claim is not etched in stone, and *should* change as often as relevant events in your life change. What may have been the correct number of allowances for you a couple of years ago may have changed since a child was born, or now that your spouse is no longer working. Maybe you bought or sold your home, or got divorced or remarried. Perhaps your child is eighteen now, has gone off to college, or is moving away from home to start a new adventure.

You should adjust your W-4 periodically as your situation warrants. *If you claim fewer allowances than you are entitled to, too much money is withheld from your paycheck.* It really is just as simple as that.

Take Back Your Tax

You have the ability to transform your W-4 into a veritable *payment gateway*, allowing your financial partner, Uncle Sam, to return your tax money to you in your paycheck every month. The average annual tax refund in the US ranges from $2,000 to $4,000. That calculates to a *potential* monthly increase in your take home pay of $167 to $333. Imagine how many credit card or auto loan payments you could make with that money—or how much you could put away in your IRA or 401-K. Please, don't just blow it on buying random "stuff."

Now let's explore how magically transform your W-4 into another type of new cashflow stream—a *payment gateway* for returning your tax money.

Meet my good friend, Mary:

Mary is a school teacher, a single mom with two kids, who makes $50,000 a year. After losing $15,000 off the top to taxes, in reality, she only takes home around $35,000. Sadly, she realizes this is not enough money to cover her family expenses, and is now ready to take action.

As a result, Mary's ultimate goal is now to take back *as much as possible* of the $15,000 she lost to income taxes. This is an aggressive goal that is challenging to achieve—but with the right financial strategy in place, it is quite possible. Correctly filling out her W-4 can increase someone in Mary's income bracket and family situation's take home pay approximately *$300 to $400 a month*, on average. That represents, potentially, another *$3,600 to $4,800 a year*!

Like most of us, Mary believed that the W-4 tracked *dependents* and assumed that allowances and dependents were the same thing. Based on this, she routinely claimed just *three (3) allowances*: one for herself and one for each of her two children. While this is certainly better than claiming one or zero, as many people have done all their lives, it is definitely not ideal for her situation.

> *For someone like Mary, a single allowance is worth, on average, from $50 to $80 a month or $600 to $960 a year. I like to be conservative and use the $50 number for hypothetical calculations like this. So let's say that the three allowances put an additional $1,800 (three allowances times $600) back into Mary's paycheck each year. Not bad, but based on her income, marital status, and financial situation, she could do a lot better.*

I will be the first to admit that reading the directions for how to correctly fill out your W-4 form can be about as exciting as watching paint dry, but I assure you *it is time well spent*. Mary is about to find this out as she goes through the process:

- *The first question instructs her to claim one (1) for herself… which she always does anyway.*
- *She has only one job, so she can claim one (1) for that.*
- *She has no spouse, so this question does not apply (-).*
- *The next question instructs her to claim one for each dependent, which, again, she always does anyway. She enters two (2).*

She is only four questions into the form and already she has identified four (4) allowances—one more than she claims now—and we are just getting warmed up.

- *Mary meets the IRS definition of head of household, so she can enter one (1) more.*
- *She will spend more than $1,900 in childcare expenses and qualifies to claim the childcare credit, so she can enter one (1) more.*

The following question pertains to child care tax credits, for which Mary also qualifies. *Note that credits are paid after the fact, just like tax refunds.* You can use your W-4 to claim allowances that put that money back into your paycheck <u>*now*</u>, when you need it most! Mary has wisely chosen to do this.

Since Mary is single, qualifies for the child care tax credit and makes less than $65,000; she can also claim two allowances for each dependent child.

She has two kids, so she can claim <u>a whopping</u> four (4) more allowances!

In case you have not been keeping score, by simply reading and understanding the W-4 form directions, Mary has been able to more than triple her allowances from **three** (3) to **ten** (10)! Do the math. *The additional seven (7) allowances will put an additional $350 a month of her own money back into her paycheck.* That is an additional $4,200 a year—$6,000 combined for all 10 allowances!

The Next Level

Now that we have picked the "low hanging fruit," things will start to get much more interesting—and challenging:

> *Mary was pleased with her $6.000 in W-4 tax savings; but she still wanted more. Even though I advised her that she would need an SBV in order to access the*

more advanced tax saving strategies, she wasn't at all sold on the idea. After all she is a teacher, not a business person. She reasoned that because teachers get summers off, it might be a good idea to get a summer job where she could earn as much as $10,000 during her break.

Mary thought this summer job would help her replace most of the $15,000 she lost to taxes at her teaching job. Good plan, right? Not really. The additional $10,000 of regular W-2 income just put her into a higher tax bracket, driving her taxable income up to $60,000 and her tax liability from $15,000 to $20,000.

The end result is that she lost half of her new income to taxes! Even worse than that, how does one measure the value of the time she lost with her kids that she used to spend with them during their summer vacation? That time is invaluable, and she will never get it back.

Suppose that instead of getting another W-2 job, Mary had chosen to start an SBV instead. What if she had focused on using it to write off many of her current expenses such as utilities, internet, cell phone service, eating out, auto mileage, travel expenses, and hiring her two kids instead of paying them allowance. This might have been the outcome:

Mary still was uncomfortable with the thought of running a business, even a part time one like an SBV. So she chose not to focus on earning additional income at this time; and she was careful to meet the minimum IRS requirements for operating a home-based business. This is a perfectly viable, conservative strategy.

To keep the metrics simple, let's say that she earned <u>no profit</u> with her SBV, but still managed to generate $10,000 in business tax deductions. In other words, she lost $10,000—on paper. Not to worry; this is where it gets good! Fortunately, because of her SBV, that $10,000 loss Mary experienced can now be written-off against her teacher's salary—thus lowering her taxable income from $50,000 to $40,000. Do you ever wonder how some businesses you just know are losing money, are somehow able to stay in business? They are probably just a link in somebody's financial chain, intended for that purpose.

In this example, her tax burden dropped from $15,000 to $12,000—that is a savings of $3,000, which amounts to a 20% decrease in her taxes for the year! Just in case you are not impressed with her tax savings, think about it like this. *In order to take home $3,000 from her job, Mary would have to earn an additional $4,500!* Am I starting to get through to you?

Of course, the above hypothetical examples and those that follow are just that—*hypothetical examples*. They should not be taken as financial guarantees of any kind. Results will vary. By implementing sound financial strategies, Mary has been able to take back $9,000 of the $15,000 of her hard-earned money lost to taxes:

1. $6,000 from correcting her W-4 tax withholding form
2. $3,000 through SBV business tax deductions

Keep in mind that the $3,000 in business tax deductions was earned just during Mary's summer break. *Had she followed this financial strategy for an entire year, one would assume she could easily have exceeded the amount of tax savings.* Later on, I will walk you step by step through some of my most lucrative SBV tax deduction strategies designed to maximize your tax savings and cashflow. But for now, let's just keep it moving.

Kudos to Mary! She has reclaimed $9,000 of her own money; so what should she do with it now? Before her newfound bounty begins to burn a hole in her pocket, she should repurpose it in such a way as to create even more cashflow. I suggested that she contact a reputable money management company and begin a strategic investment program.

She Looks Like A Million Dollars

Let's use Mary again to illustrate this concept in action…

> *Mary has $30,000 in consumer debt and makes monthly principal and interest payments totaling $750 to service that debt. To keep things simple, let's say the debt comprises a $15,000 car note and $15,000 in credit card debt. In the real world, this debt might also include things such as student loans, medical loans, and other types of high interest borrowing.*

Mary, like many of us, is struggling to live comfortably on what she makes and also be able to save for retirement. She has corrected her W-4, started an SBV, and is now working from a *Sword and Shield* mindset. By combining her tax savings, business deductions, and any incremental income generated by her SBV, she has created an additional $1,100 a month of new cashflow to allocate toward debt elimination.

> *For simplicity's sake, and to spare us both a migraine, I will skip the complicated mathematical calculations and "if-then-else" contingency scenarios that went into this example.*

> *Mary used her cashflow to attack her smallest debts, first, like credit cards, for example. Eliminating*

these small debts frees up cashflow to apply toward larger ones like auto loans second mortgages and student loans. Once these larger debts are eliminated, even more cashflow is freed up. Let's just say that by taking this proven successful strategic approach, and by staying on track, Mary's debt will be totally eliminated in 20 months!

Mary now has freed up $1,850 monthly cashflow with which to begin a long overdue investment program. Where did that number come from? *It is the aggregate of the $750 a month she was paying before and the $1,100 of new cashflow generated from tax savings, business deductions, and incremental income* produced by her SBV. Don't be intimidated. No one expects you to be a professional investor. In fact, I strongly suggest that you don't even try. Instead, I suggest that you sign on with one of the top money management companies I mentioned earlier, and let them do the heavy lifting for you. They are quite good at it.

With $1,850 a month of new cash flow to invest at a conservative 8% annual ROI, Mary would have in her investment portfolio:

- $207,000 in seven years.
- $444,000 in twelve years.

- $1,089,000 in twenty years.

This, of course, would be in addition to any Social Security, 401k, or other retirement pension such as what she might get from her school or another employer.

That is right…Mary could be a millionaire in just 20 years on a teacher's salary!

The interest from a million dollars is around $8,500 a month, depending on market conditions. Based on what she makes now, I suspect she could live quite comfortably on that, don't you? In any instance, Mary would be able to retire on more money than she currently makes as a teacher, if she puts her personal financial success strategy in place now… and so can you!

Mary has now been introduced to the most traditional and widely accepted wealth building concept in the financial world—*cash-asset-cash*. She has learned to take cash, invest it into revenue generating assets; which will, in turn, generate more cash. This is the polar opposite of the *Cycle of Pain* we discussed earlier.

NOTES

CHAPTER 6
HOW TAX DEDUCTIONS REALLY WORK

"I am proud to be paying taxes in the United States. The only thing is I could be just as proud for half of the money."
ARTHUR GODFREY

How much "cash in your pocket" is a tax deduction really worth? Unlike tax credits, tax deductions are *not* a dollar for dollar exchange. *A $1,000 tax deduction, for example, does not put $1,000 back in your pocket.* If you are in a 30% tax bracket, it would actually return around $300 dollars to you, which is, roughly, the amount of tax you would have paid on that money.

Tax deductions are calculated taking variables into consideration such as your tax bracket and whether it is W-2, 1099, or investment income that is involved.

> *The primary advantage of tax deductions is that they reduce your amount of <u>taxable</u> income, which translates into you paying less tax—putting more cash in your pocket. You will recall me saying that "the SBV is not all about earning more income; it is about making less of your job income taxable." The SBV creates new cashflow by converting everyday expenses, money that you were going to spend anyway, into lucrative tax deductions.*

To me, the best thing about tax deductions is that they can be *converted into allowances* and used to get your money back into your paycheck each month instead of having to wait a year for a tax refund. Remember in the example where Mary corrected her W-4 and was able to claim two allowances per dependent child because she qualified for the Childcare Tax Credit? She used her W-4 to convert that credit into allowances, and get the money back in her check every month as opposed to waiting until she filed her taxes.

Driving Miss Daisy To The Bank

One of the most beneficial tax deductions available through your SBV is the *auto mileage deduction*. A day does not go by that you don't hear someone complain about the high price of gasoline. In my area, it currently fluctuates between $3.50 and $4.00 a gallon. Let's put this in perspective:

- If you have a 20-gallon tank, it would cost you around $80 to fill up your gas tank.
- If you got 20 miles per gallon, you would be able to drive 400 miles on a tank of gas.
- This equates to about 20 cents a mile that you would pay for gas under these circumstances.

- The current IRS standard mileage reimbursement rate is 55 cents a mile (soon to be 57.5 cents).
- That means that you make 35 cents profit for every mile you drive for business purposes.

Another way to look at it is that Uncle Sam pays you $35 for every 100 miles you drive for business purposes! If, for example, you drive 20,000 miles this year; and half of those can be considered business miles—that's a $3,500 tax deduction!

The key to making the mileage deduction work for you is to translate trips you would take *anyway* into business miles through your SBV. *Don't drive extra miles just to have something to write off;* that would be counterproductive. You would actually be spending more than you would save. Again, this strategy is completely legal and is recognized and accepted by the IRS as long as it is done with *integrity* and *transparency*. How is this accomplished? I am glad you asked.

> *Suppose during one of your routine trips to run errands, you decided to meet a friend at a restaurant for lunch. Instead of limiting your conversation to the usual mindless chitchat, you tell your friend about your SBV and how it helps you lower your taxes and debt and build business and retirement income. Voila!*

Your casual lunch just became a business lunch, and 50% of it can be deducted through your SBV.

Or maybe you are dining out alone and you just happen to strike up a conversation with the person at the table next to you, or with someone as you are waiting in line to be seated. Talk about your business venture, give them a business card (be sure to get theirs for documentation of the meeting, or at least get their name and contact information), and you have once again created a deductible business expense.

I cannot overemphasize the importance of documentation and good tax recordkeeping. You need to make it a habit to capture the name of the person you met or ate with, keep a copy of the meal receipt, and record your starting and ending auto mileage in order to have bullet-proof documentation to support your claim. The better you get at transforming everyday expenses into business deductions, the more of your hard-earned tax dollars you can reclaim. Take back your tax!

There Is No Place Like Home

The *office in the home* is fundamental to an effective strategic business venture strategy. Note that this is different from your itemized home mortgage interest deduction. You claim the former on your

1040 Schedule A. The office in the home is claimed on your Schedule C. Your home is usually your largest expense, *except for taxes* of course; therefore, it provides tremendous opportunity for generating new cashflow through tax deductions.

This particular deduction is somewhat more complicated than many of the other deductions because it requires you to calculate the total square footage of your home, as well as the square footage used as your *home office*. Next, you must factor that calculation proportionately by the amount of your mortgage payment. Yes, this can be a pain; but, I promise you, you will be glad you made the effort when you see the financial benefit.

Additionally, you have a number of services in your home that can be utilized in your SBV and written off accordingly; things such as *utilities, internet, telephone, electronics, computers,* furniture, *equipment, housekeeping,* and more. All of these are based either on the percentage of square footage your office occupies in the home or the percentage of usage of the item by the business. Individually, they are not that significant, but collectively—can you say *"cha-ching?"*

If you are a renter, the *office in the home deduction* is a no-brainer. Renters are the redheaded stepchildren of the tax code; they get almost no tax breaks from the IRS. This strategy allows you to deduct the percentage of the total square footage allocated to your SBV as well as the other associated home-based expenses, similarly to how it is done with a mortgaged home. Renters, don't sleep on this one.

If Ya Gotta Go, Ya Gotta Go!

If you love to travel, and who doesn't, then you should definitely learn how to use your SBV to write off trips and vacations. If you own rental real estate, you are probably aware that you can write off transportation, food, and other costs related to visiting, maintaining and checking on your property. The *business travel deduction* works much the same way.

It is easy to turn a vacation cruise into a business trip. For example, just allocate some of the time on the ship, or on the island, or at dinner, or at the show to discuss your business. Be sure to collect names and contact information on the people you discussed business with, keep receipts from the trip, or set up a business meeting with a prospective client at your destination point. Just remember to document, document, document; it is worth the effort.

Your SBV allows you to proportionately claim all

necessary expenses during the travel experience. That includes the following:

- Travel by air, bus, car, cab, train, or other vehicle between your home and the business destination
- All expenses incurred by your personal vehicle while you were at a business destination, including tolls, parking meters, and gas
- Any food that you need during your trip
- Any accommodation that you need during your trip
- All tips given to staff during travel
- All dry cleaning and laundry bills
- Phone calls during your business trip

It is not unusual to spend $2,000 or more on a vacation trip. If that same trip were claimed as a business trip, again assuming a 30% tax rate, $600 dollars would find its way back into your pocket through tax savings. If you were going to take this trip anyway, that is $600 dollars that can go into <u>your</u> pocket instead of Uncle Sam's. The beauty of this deduction is that you were going to take this trip or vacation anyway. After all, if you gotta go, you gotta go!

Another Day, Another Quarter

If, like me, you are a parent who pays his child a weekly or monthly allowance, it might surprise you to know just how much this actually costs you. If you really want a cold slap in the face, just calculate how much you need to earn, before taxes, in order to pay that allowance. It is easy to do—just add approximately 30% to what you pay your child in allowance.

> *Are you mad yet? Well don't get mad; get an SBV! I know that doesn't rhyme—but I think you get the point.*

First of all, don't you have better things to do with 30% of your hard earned money than to give it to Uncle Sam? How about putting it away in a college fund for your child's future education or using it to pay down your credit card balances?

Your SBV allows you to shield that income from excessive taxation by giving you a vehicle to hire your six- to eighteen-year-old child and pay him/her a *salary* instead of an allowance—up to $6,200 a year per child! That's right, you can legally do this. IRS rules and regulations apply, of course.

To take advantage of this significant but seldom utilized tax deduction, simply develop a job description for your new "employee" with real responsibilities that are applicable to your business and within the capabilities of your child. Be sure that the job pays a reasonable wage based on those responsibilities.

> *For example, a pre-teen is certainly capable of opening your mail, answering your business line, posting regularly to your social media accounts, performing clerical duties, and researching information online.*

This is not a game—so this strategy is not to be taken lightly. It can put real money back in your pocket, but, again transparency and documentation are required by the IRS. A bit more tangible structure must be put in place as well in order to maximize this strategy and protect you from being accused of fraud. For example, it will be necessary to set up a separate bank account in which to deposit the funds paid to your child.

Make sure there is a clear and transparent paper trail when the money is withdrawn from the account. *Please—do not get caught with your hand in the cookie jar on this one!* If you think all this sounds like too much trouble, perhaps this deduction is not for you. However, before you throw the baby out with the bath water, just take a minute and do the math—you may change your mind.

Stick Out Your Tongue And Say... Ahhhhh

Health insurance presents another great tax deductible opportunity. Did you know that you can deduct *unreimbursed* or *out-of-pocket* medical premiums, prescription medications, and other costs through your SBV? There are, however, several kinds of insurance that are not tax deductible. Make sure that you find out what *does* and what *does not* apply to your particular situation.

I am sure that, on occasion, you have had to choose health insurance policies that were less expensive and provided less than ideal coverage and protection in order to save money. Through your SBV, you can lower your health insurance costs considerably. As you get older, medical expenses grow, and you may find yourself unable to afford the treatment you need.

> *Using the SBV strategy, you have access to previously inaccessible options that can make health care more affordable for you and your family.*

There are more than 400 business tax deductions available to home-based business owners. Your SBV gives you access to all of these, but, in reality, *you will probably only need to use six to eight of them to accomplish your goal*. I have given you the briefest of examples of some you may wish to consider.

NOTES

CHAPTER 7
THE JOB ISN'T OVER UNTIL THE PAPERWORK IS DONE

"You don't pay taxes... they take taxes."
CHRIS ROCK

The average person hates talking about taxes. It really creeps them out. For that reason, *this is by far the shortest chapter in the book*. I promise you, it won't hurt—much!

The culmination of this slow dance with Uncle Sam occurs on or around April 15th when we file our income tax returns. For many it is a time of sadness because they owe taxes; for others, it is a time of great anticipation as they await their fat tax refund check. *For me, it is a time of great excitement* because I find out just how much of my hard earned tax money I was able to take back from the IRS; and how much it had earned me through my investments.

Most people don't prepare their own income tax returns. It can be intimidating, to say the least. It's so much easier to just pay some reputable tax preparer to do it for you. If all you are after is a tax refund check, then this is a viable option for you. However, if you plan to utilize the strategies outlined in this book, this would be a big mistake. If you are *in it to win it*, I suggest you find a CPA or tax preparation specialist who is knowledgeable about home based business tax laws; after all, that is essentially what an SBV is, as far as Uncle Sam is concerned.

Explain to your tax preparer that you want to take home as much money in your paycheck each month as possible, so that you can use it to pay bills, lower debt and invest. *He or she will probably look at you with newfound respect.* Also make sure that you thoroughly understand the Schedule A and Schedule C sections of your 1040 Tax Form... this, my friend is where the bulk of your tax deductions reside.

The Form 1040 Schedule A

You may be somewhat familiar with this form. As a wage earning employee, this is probably the only section where you can catch a break. This is where you can claim your itemized deductions, such as:

1. Medical and Dental Expenses
2. Interest You Paid
3. Gifts to Charity
4. Casualty and Theft Losses
5. Job Expenses
6. Certain Miscellaneous Deductions.

If you aren't at least filing a Schedule A, then you might as well bend over, grab your ankles and ask Uncle Sam to be gentle!

The Form 1040 Schedule C

This form can be your best friend if you have an SBV. This is where you record your profit or loss from business. This is where one accounts for all those business venture expenses that will provide tax relief to your beleaguered job income. Of course, 1099 income is also tracked here; but this is much less of a focus for you initially.

I introduce *revenue generation strategies* to my clients after they have *maxed out business expense conversions* and / or have begun making so much 1099 income that they need <u>all</u> of their tax deductions to shield it. When this happens, you may as well go for it, because there is nothing left to shield your job income. I assume that earning too much money is not a problem for you!

That's it... we're done here. I hope you paid attention because if you didn't, your chances of becoming a nonprofit millionaire go down significantly.

NOTES

CHAPTER 8

CHOOSING YOUR SBV

"Most people don't recognize opportunity when it comes, because it is usually dressed in overalls and looks like work."
THOMAS ALVA EDISON

So… once you commit to having a Strategic Business Venture in your life, how do you choose one that is just right for you? When choosing an SBV, or a traditional job for that matter, always remember something that is well worth repeating: "If it is not your passion, don't make it your profession!" People who love what they do, never work a day in their lives.

I suggest that you choose an SBV related to something you enjoy doing, are very good at, and are going to spend time doing anyway. Given the extremely demanding and unpredictable work schedules of nonprofit and social sector professionals, this is imperative. Personally, I chose to be an author; and it has worked extremely well for me so far. I love to read and write; and I have never been a big product person. I am not good at making things, and even worse at selling them afterward. If you feel that way as well, don't feel bad. Only 3% of the population enjoy sales and are good at it. I wish I had that rare skill—proficient sales professionals make a lot of money!

As an author I focus on *monetizing my intellectual property*. I can sell books, consult with clients, and/or provide cashflow management coaching through my *SBV Academy Online*. You will hear much more about the Academy later. Intellectual property doesn't require manufacturing, warehousing, or other similar hard costs. There is no product wear and tear, shrinkage or employee theft. The best part is that I can work from the comfort and convenience of my own home in my spare time—minimizing potential conflicts with my "real" job.

Generally speaking, I would advise most people to consider some type of *consulting business* an SBV. Most people are experts at <u>something</u>... in their own mind, anyway. The ultimate thrill for me is to get paid well for something that exists only in my head. If you are someone that others often come to for advice or guidance, either at work or in your personal life—you should consider being a part time consultant in your field of expertise. You're going to give advice anyway; why not get paid for it?

Sometimes you become an expert out of necessity. I became a *cashflow management expert* when a bitter divorce cost me half of my retirement pension—followed by the realization that I would never be able to replace what I had lost in the time remaining before retirement. The thought of not being able to retire on time, or possibly having to work a job until the day I die, inspired me to pursue the financial education necessary to get back on my feet. It turned out to be a blessing in disguise because my quest for financial knowledge led me to develop the Strategic Business Venture, and start my own consulting business.

It isn't necessary that you make a lot of money consulting because, remember, *the SBV is not about earning more income, it is about making less of your job income taxable.* Anyway, who knows how long it will take before you actually secure a paying client; but with your SBV, tax deductions can begin providing financial relief immediately.

> *A little-known fact is that the average person in business, during the first couple of years, will generate more net positive cash flow through tax savings than through product sales!*

The ability to manage losses is every bit as important as the ability to manage profit; perhaps even more so. Business losses can be converted to lucrative tax deductions in certain circumstances, as long as you are doing business with the *"intent to make a profit."* Is this a loophole? Of course it is—a perfectly legal one that the wealthy have taken advantage of since forever. If this tactic is fair game for them, then it is fair game for you. I call this *"equal stretch."* Of course there are some legal obligations that must be fulfilled first; but how is that different from any other significant occurrence in your life?

Not to worry, the qualification process and logistics of setting up a consulting based SBV is not difficult. *As my client, I will walk you through the initial phases of start-up, implementation and ongoing operation until you get the hang of it.* Once you have chosen your SBV, a whole new world will open up to you—a world filled with new challenges and opportunities. For a few hours a week, you will function as an entrepreneur; a completely different mindset from that of a wage earning employee. The rules of entrepreneurship are really quite simple: *You kill what you eat. If you don't kill anything—you do not eat anything!*

No tax saving strategies, regardless of how brilliant, will help you if you don't implement them. You take your paycheck at work for granted because it comes to you every month on autopilot. It may not be enough, but at least you can count on it. *Unfortunately, tax deductions don't work like that.* You must work your SBV diligently over the long term in order to reap the financial benefits—no pain, no gain.

Firing Your Boss

It's not entirely out of the question to believe that a hobby or part time business venture could eventually grow to the point that it replaces your job as your primary source of income. *It happens more often than you might think.* It is no secret that most people hate their jobs, and the only reason they show up to work every day is to collect a paycheck. They would like nothing better than to tell their boss to: "take this job and shove it!"

Conversely, the SBV is designed for people who actually like their jobs, and don't want to quit. *Its purpose is to strategically shield and protect your job income from excessive taxation. Any ancillary income produced is considered a bonus.* However, I have seen SBVs thrive to the point that people have walked away from their old jobs. We all face many possible futures. For example, my first book, "Nonprofit Doesn't Mean No Profit," was an Amazon #1 best seller. Sure, I made a little money from book sales; but I actually made much more from speaking engagements and personal coaching. As intended, the primary benefit was tax savings, and debt reduction.

But what if my book had sold millions of copies and become a New York Times best seller instead?

Imagine if the manuscript was made into a movie, starring some big name Hollywood actor, and it became a box office smash. Odds are I would have made enough money to quit my job if I wanted to, and buy a red convertible sports car or a luxurious mansion somewhere. Hey, it could happen. Should that bizarre scenario have occurred, perhaps I would have been motivated to "fire my boss," but because I truly love working in the nonprofit world, I would probably have just joined the Board and become a major donor instead!

My point is that it *is* quite possible to generate significant income with an SBV; *perhaps enough to eventually equal or replace your current job income.* Once the basic "minimize taxes, eliminate debt and invest" strategies have been mastered, there are other more advanced financial strategies available that demonstrate how this can be accomplished. By the way, I teach these advanced strategies to my cashflow management coaching clients prior to completion of their instruction.

Again, income generation is not the intended focus of the SBV… but I'm sure you won't be mad if it happens!

NOTES

CHAPTER 9

THE SBV ACADEMY ONLINE

"I am always doing that which I cannot do… in order that I may learn how to do it."
PABLO PICASSO

You can learn a lot from reading self-help books, watching instructional videos, and attending workshops and seminars; but the best way to learn all about the *Strategic Business Venture* is through the **SBV Academy Online**. We all learn best in a supportive coaching environment; and this is exactly what the Academy provides.

> *"The SBV Academy will show you how to bring more money home in your paycheck... without working longer hours, getting a second job or begging your boss for a raise. You will learn how to pay less in taxes, get out of debt and free up money to invest in the future."*

In other words, the SBV Academy Online will prepare you to become a nonprofit millionaire!

At the Academy, all the secrets and financial strategies associated with the SBV will be revealed. You will receive expert coaching on how to set up, start, manage and successfully operate your own SBV; as well as guidance in identifying and effectively utilizing tax deductions appropriate for your particular situation and circumstances.

Initially, I was "old school;" meeting clients for coaching sessions at local restaurants and trendy entrepreneur gathering spots after work hours and on weekends. *Anywhere there was Wi-Fi I could do a presentation or a coaching session.* True to the SBV strategy, I reasoned that since I was going to have to eat anyway... why not make my breakfast, lunch or dinner a business expense and write it off? Eventually, however, *logistical and capacity challenges* took their toll, rendering this strategy less and less effective.

Then along came the internet—and everything changed! I can now coach more clients online than would be possible face to face; all in my free time, from the comfort and convenience of my own home—without sacrificing the all-important *personal touch*. By incorporating the latest online meeting and presentation systems, as well as other high-tech software into my coaching repertoire; I can now do live and automated webinars, screen sharing, Google Hangouts and can transform standard PowerPoint presentations into "neuro-linguistic" video masterpieces.

As the SBV Academy Online curriculum expands, I can now provide cashflow management services in both *Personal Coaching* and *Small Group Coaching* formats; as well as via my new video-based coaching program called *"The Magic of the SBV."* Each provides similar instructional content delivered in the manner most comfortable to the client. Following is a detailed description of each.

Level One Coaching

In Level One, we begin at the beginning.

There are three basic *secrets to financial success*: a) minimizing your taxes, b) getting out of debt and c) freeing up money to invest in the future. Level One is where we begin to address these key issues:

1. I will walk you step by step through the process of correcting your *W-4 Tax Withholding Form* for maximum effectiveness; returning as much money as possible to your paycheck each month.

2. You will learn to create *new cashflow streams* from tax savings and debt reduction which can be utilized in any number of ways to improve your financial situation.

3. You will be trained on a simple, easy to use financial software called the *Cashflow Manager* that will make tracking, documenting and reporting tax deductible expenses a snap.

4. We will conduct a *Current State/Future State*

Financial Analysis that will identify exactly when you want to retire, and how much money you will need to support your desired lifestyle when you do.

5. Once your financial goals are established, I will work with you to design a detailed, comprehensive action plan to achieve them.

Level Two Coaching

The *Current State/Future State Financial Analysis* conducted in Level One Coaching makes it clear to most people that they simply *"can't get there from here."* I am, of course, referring to their plan to retire on schedule at the income level desired. It will either take them longer than anticipated to get there or they will not have enough money to maintain their desired lifestyle when they do. In a *worst case scenario*, they may find themselves unable to retire at all.

Resolving issues related to both your current state and future state can be addressed by effective utilization of the Strategic Business Venture strategy. Level Two Coaching is all about learning and implementing financial strategies based on the tax advantages provided by the SBV:

1. I will help you determine which business category works best for your SBV; typically a sole proprietorship, LLC or S-Corp (under certain circumstances) will work best.
2. You will learn how to register your SBV with the IRS, obtain an official EIN number and establish a business bank account needed to document SBV related income and expenses.
3. Depending on the type of SBV you choose for yourself, I will coach you on how to develop and monetize marketable products, services and intellectual property to establish legitimacy.
4. Once all this is in place we will select and train you on several tax deduction strategies that will allow you to reclaim most if not all of the money you lose to income taxes each year.
5. I will introduce you to the concept of "Cash-Asset-Cash," the bedrock principle for building generational wealth; and train you on its practical application with the SBV.

Level Three Coaching

At this level, you will be eligible to become a *full business partner in my own personal SBV*. Only individuals who have successfully completed Level One and Level Two will be considered. At this level, you will be trained to actually *do what I do*; teach others how to: 1) Minimize their taxes, 2) Get out of debt and 3) Invest for the future.

For the record, you can definitely transform yourself into a *nonprofit millionaire* by only using techniques from Level One and Level Two—it will just take you longer to get there. *The main thing you learn in Level Three Coaching is how to quickly generate lots of 1099 income.* The combination of minimizing your taxes and debt, combined with 1099 income generation is powerful; and can greatly accelerate your progress toward nonprofit millionaire status.

Video Coaching Program

If all the Level One, Level Two and Level Three stuff seems like a bit much, perhaps my video coaching program, *"The Magic of the SBV"* is more your style. Though not as comprehensive as the other coaching options, for some people it is just enough to keep the strategies top of mind. Here's how it works:

1. A private online membership portal with password protected access is established for you.

2. Each week for several weeks, a new instructional video featuring different aspects of the Strategic Business Venture strategy is uploaded to your portal.

3. The videos were created from actual PowerPoint presentations used in Level One and Level Two Coaching sessions.

4. Once in your private portal, videos are available to you at your convenience.

5. Videos in your portal are automatically updated as newer versions of those videos become available.

6. One on one coaching sessions with me can also be purchased through your private portal.

NOTES

For information on how you can enroll in the SBV Academy Online for: 1) *Personal Coaching,* 3) *Small Group Coaching,* or 3) *The Magic of the SBV* video coaching course:

Call Us Toll Free at...
1-877-223-0346
Your first phone consultation is free!

Or visit our website at...
www.sbvacademyonline.com

CONCLUSION

SWORD & SHIELD MINDSET

"Strategy without tactics is the slowest route to victory. Tactics without strategy is the noise before defeat."
SUN TZU, THE ART OF WAR

The Sword & Shield is not a tactic, or a strategy, or even a system; it is a mindset—a way of translating thought into action. It is not to be confused with conditions like the *Cycle of Pain* or processes like my *Three Steps to Financial Success*. It does not diminish or replace either; instead, it synergistically binds them together. The idea came to me after watching a late night documentary on the gladiators of ancient Rome. The film was based on the life and death combat strategies and battle tactics employed in the arena by ancient gladiators.

Envision, if you will, the gladiators of ancient Rome. They carried a *mighty sword for offense* and a *sturdy shield for defense*. They depended primarily on their powerful swords to ensure their survival in the arena. Their shields, however, were used mostly as a defensive measure when their sword attack was unsuccessful or when they were caught off balance or out of position.

What do you suppose would happen to a gladiator if his *only sword* broke in combat? In preparation for this catastrophic possibility, they all carried a shield and a backup weapon like a short sword or dagger to fall back on. Having a *Plan-B* is just *good common sense*, right? Then why do so many nonprofit and social sector professionals have no financial fallback position? Why do they depend exclusively on their jobs to provide for themselves and their families? Perhaps Frank Lloyd Wright was correct when he said, "There is nothing more uncommon than common sense."

Like the gladiator's sword, your job income is, no doubt, the primary weapon in your day-to-day battle for financial survival. What would happen to you and your family if, for whatever reason, you suddenly or unexpectedly lost your job? Do you have a *shield* or a *Plan B* to fall back on? This grim reality check planted the seeds in my mind that would eventually become the *Strategic Business Venture*. The SBV provides a *shield* for your job income; and can, potentially, become a *sword* in its own right should your job unexpectedly go away.

This *Sword and Shield* mindset works well for people who, unlike most Americans, genuinely like their jobs and want to keep them. They are <u>not</u> in such a hurry to "fire their boss" or to get in on "the next big thing." However, they still desperately need to reduce their taxes and debt. If you are one of those people, your objective should be pretty straightforward. You must acknowledge that Uncle Sam is taking too much money from you in taxes; *much less* than he is taking from people who make a lot more than you do. More importantly, however, you must consign yourself to take action to correct this situation. *Uncle Sam is going to get his tax money from somebody—you just want to make sure that he doesn't get it all from you.*

REFERENCES

2013 Form W-4 - Internal Revenue Service. www.irs.gov/pub/irs-pdf/fw4.pdf

Day, Edward. Quotes on Wealth, Success, and All Things Money. http://www.invest-safely.com/quotes-on-wealth.html

Edison, Thomas Alva. Quotes. http://www.attraxionarts.com/articles/overall-success/152-law-of-attraction-part-3-recognition-and-response

Einstein, Albert. Theory of relativity. Wikipedia. http://en.wikipedia.org/wiki/Theory_of_relativity

Friedman, Milton. Goodreads, http://www.goodreads.com/author/quotes/5001.Milton_Friedman

Getty, Jean Paul. Searchquotes, http://www.searchquotes.com/search/Jean_Paul_Getty_Residual_Income/

Home-based Business, http://www.sba.gov/content/home-based-businesses

Jim Rohn Quotes. http://thinkexist.com/quotation/formal_education_will_make_you_a_living-self/13803.html

Internal Revenue Services. www.irs.gov/pub/irs-pdf/p919.pdf

Khurana, Simran. Tax Quotes, http://quotations.about.com/od/moretypes/a/taxquotes1.htm

Longley, Robert. Why Small Businesses Fail: SBA, http://usgovinfo.about.com/od/smallbusiness/a/whybusfail.htm

Mieville, China. Quotes. http://www.experiencefestival.com/china_mieville

Millionaire. Wikipedia. https://en.wikipedia.org/wiki/Millionaire

Money quotes. http://www.limunltd.com/numismatica/trivia/

Rockefeller, John D. http://quotationsbook.com/quote/12110/

Rogers, Will. Tax Quotes. http://quotations.about.com/od/moretypes/a/taxquotes1.htm

Roth, JD. The Seven Enemies of Financial Success, http://www.getrichslowly.org/blog/2009/08/25/the-seven-enemies-of-financial-success/

Tax. Wikipedia. http://en.wikipedia.org/wiki/Tax

Tax Quotes. http://www.quotegarden.com/taxes.html

Tim. American Household Credit Card Debt Statistics: 2013, http://www.nerdwallet.com/blog/credit-card-data/average-credit-card-debt-household/

Tzu, Sun. *The Art of War*. Thomas Cleary (Translator)

US Consumer Debt Statistics and Trends 2012, http://visual.ly/us-consumer-debt-statistics-and-trends-2012

Weltman, Barbara. Home-Based Business Tax Deductions: 5 Things You Need To Know, http://www.huffingtonpost.com/2011/04/05/home-based-business-tax-deductions-5-things_n_915039.html

Made in the USA
San Bernardino, CA
26 April 2015